SandCastle

Word Families Set 6

-unk as in skunk

Pam Scheunemann

Consulting Editor Monica Marx, M.A./Reading Specialist

ABDO
Publishing Company

Published by SandCastle™, an imprint of ABDO Publishing Company, 4940 Viking Drive, Edina, Minnesota 55435.

Printed in the United States.

Credits
Edited by: Pam Price
Curriculum Coordinator: Nancy Tuminelly
Cover and Interior Design and Production: Mighty Media
Photo Credits: Brand X Pictures, Corbis Images, Corel, Hemera, PhotoDisc, Stockbyte

Library of Congress Cataloging-in-Publication Data

Scheunemann, Pam, 1955-
    -Unk as in skunk / Pam Scheunemann.
    p. cm. -- (Word families. Set VI)
    Summary: Introduces, in brief text and illustrations, the use of the letter combination "unk" in such words as "skunk," "chunk," "dunk," and "trunk."
    ISBN 1-59197-259-0
    1. Readers (Primary) [1. Vocabulary. 2. Reading.] I. Title.

PE1119 .S4355 2003
428.1--dc21   2002038221

SandCastle™ books are created by a professional team of educators, reading specialists, and content developers around five essential components that include phonemic awareness, phonics, vocabulary, text comprehension, and fluency. All books are written, reviewed, and leveled for guided reading, early intervention reading, and Accelerated Reader® programs and designed for use in shared, guided, and independent reading and writing activities to support a balanced approach to literacy instruction.

Let Us Know

After reading the book, SandCastle would like you to tell us your stories about reading. What is your favorite page? Was there something hard that you needed help with? Share the ups and downs of learning to read. We want to hear from you! To get posted on the ABDO Publishing Company Web site, send us email at:

sandcastle@abdopub.com

SandCastle Level: Beginning

-unk Words

bunk

dunk

junk

skunk

sunk

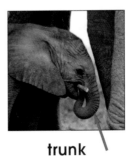

trunk

3

Freddy sits on the
bottom bunk.

Mrs. Smith likes to dunk
a cookie in her coffee.

Diane has a lot of junk
in her locker.

The skunk is by the river.

The ship has sunk in the water.

A baby elephant has a
small trunk.

The Skunk in the Trunk

Mark had a car
with a lot of spunk.

It looked better than his friend Bob's hunk of junk.

But when he drove,
it went clunk, clunk!

Then he heard
another noise,
plunk, plunk!
He got out
to look in the trunk.

15

There it was,
a big old skunk.

Boy, oh boy,
that trunk stunk!

He took the car to the lake
to give it a dunk.

The skunk
jumped from
the trunk.

Oh, no, the whole thing just sunk!

That was the
end of the car,
but not the
skunk!

The -unk Word Family

bunk	junk
chunk	plunk
clunk	shrunk
drunk	skunk
dunk	spunk
flunk	stunk
gunk	sunk
hunk	trunk

Glossary

Some of the words in this list may have more than one meaning. The meaning listed here reflects the way the word is used in the book.

dunk   to dip something into a liquid

spunk   lively and full of energy

sunk   past tense of sink; to fall or drop to a lower level

trunk   an elephant's long nose; the large storage compartment in the back of a car

About SandCastle™

A professional team of educators, reading specialists, and content developers created the SandCastle™ series to support young readers as they develop reading skills and strategies and increase their general knowledge. The SandCastle™ series has four levels that correspond to early literacy development in young children. The levels are provided to help teachers and parents select the appropriate books for young readers.

Emerging Readers
(no flags)

Beginning Readers
(1 flag)

Transitional Readers
(2 flags)

Fluent Readers
(3 flags)

These levels are meant only as a guide. All levels are subject to change.

To see a complete list of SandCastle™ books and other nonfiction titles from ABDO Publishing Company, visit www.abdopub.com or contact us at:

4940 Viking Drive, Edina, Minnesota 55435 • 1-800-800-1312 • fax: 1-952-831-1632